D0768665

Main

Energy in the Real World

by Christine Zuchora-Walske

Content Consultant
Dr. Tony Borgerding
Professor of Chemistry
University of St. Thomas

CORE
LIBRARY

Published by ABDO Publishing Company, PO Box 398166, Minneapolis,
MN 55439. Copyright © 2013 by Abdo Consulting Group, Inc.
International copyrights reserved in all countries. No part of this book may
be reproduced in any form without written permission from the publisher.
The Core Library™ is a trademark and logo of ABDO Publishing Company.

Printed in the United States of America,
North Mankato, Minnesota
112012
012013

♻ THIS BOOK CONTAINS AT LEAST 10% RECYCLED MATERIALS.

Editor: Karen Latchana Kenney
Series Designer: Becky Daum

Cataloging-in-Publication Data
Zuchora-Walske, Christine.
 Energy in the real world / Christine Zuchora-Walske.
   p. cm. -- (Science in the real world)
Includes bibliographical references and index.
ISBN 978-1-61783-739-5
1. Energy--Juvenile literature.   I. Title.
531/.6--dc21
                                                2012946828

Photo Credits: Shutterstock Images, cover, 1, 4, 20, 28, 30, 41, 45; Jacek
Chabraszewski/Shutterstock Images, 8; Time Life Pictures/Getty Images,
10; Red Line Editorial, 15, 21; AP Images, 16; FlashStudio/Shutterstock
Images, 18; Kyodo/AP Images, 23; Larisa Lofitskaya/Shutterstock Images,
24; Carolina K. Smith, M.D./Shutterstock Images, 33; Kotenko Oleksandr/
Shutterstock Images, 34; Sander van der Werf/Shutterstock Images, 36

CONTENTS

CHAPTER ONE
Energy Basics 4

CHAPTER TWO
**How Do We Know
about Energy?** 10

CHAPTER THREE
Kinetic Energy 18

CHAPTER FOUR
Potential Energy 24

CHAPTER FIVE
Sunlight: Earth's Engine 30

CHAPTER SIX
Motion into Megawatts 36

Important Dates 42
Other Ways You Can Find Energy
in the Real World 43
Stop and Think .44
Glossary 46
Learn More 47
Index 48
About the Author 48

Energy Basics

Energy is amazing. It's the engine that drives our universe. Energy makes things happen.

Energy is the ability to do work. It is also the ability to change matter. In fact, energy exists within all matter. It's in the book in your hand and the sun overhead. It's in the ground you walk on and the food you eat. It's in every living and nonliving thing—including you!

Energy is in everything—from the book in your hands to the tree you lean against.

Energy takes two main forms. Kinetic energy is motion. Potential energy is energy that has not yet been used. We sometimes call potential energy stored energy.

Energy is always conserved. That means energy cannot be created or destroyed. It can only change type or location. When energy changes from one type into another or moves from one place to another, energy transfer occurs. Every time things interact, they transfer some energy.

Energy Conservation

The term *energy conservation* has two meanings. One meaning explains how energy behaves. It changes as it is released or used. The term also means using energy as efficiently as possible. As energy is used, some changes into another useful form. The rest escapes into the environment. In an efficient transfer, not much energy is lost into the environment.

Energy All Around Us

Energy is at work all around us. You can observe it working at any moment of any day, no matter where you are.

Let's say you're at your local park. You're sitting under a tree watching the world go by.

You look up into a tree. Its branches are waving in the breeze. The moving air has kinetic energy. The breeze transfers some of its energy to the tree branches.

You look around the park. A community garden full of vegetables is in a sunny spot. A family is weeding their plot and picking cherry tomatoes. The sunlight shining on the plants has energy. The plants change the sun's light energy into chemical energy. The plants use some of that chemical energy to grow. They store the rest in their leaves and fruits.

The family eats a picnic. It includes the tomatoes. Food contains chemical energy. When the child eats the food, it releases some of its energy into her body. Her body converts the food's chemical energy into kinetic energy.

The child sits at the top of the slide for a moment. While she sits at the top of the slide, she has potential

Potential energy changes to kinetic energy as a child goes down a slide.

energy. When she pushes herself, she releases that energy. It changes into motion and carries her to the ground.

The more you look around, the more energy you see, hear, and feel. You can tell that energy is everywhere. And it's always on the move.

Richard Feynman was a famous scientist who studied physics. In his book *Surely You're Joking Mr. Feynman!*, he discusses how energy is a small word for all of the things it can do. He wrote:

> There was a book that started out with four pictures: first there was a wind-up toy; then there was an automobile; then there was a boy riding a bicycle; then there was something else. And underneath each picture it said, "What makes it go?"
>
> . . . I turned the page. The answer was, for the wind-up toy, "Energy makes it go." And for the boy on the bicycle, "Energy makes it go." For everything, "Energy makes it go."
>
> Now that doesn't mean anything . . . it's just a word!
>
> What they should have done is to look at the wind-up toy, see that there are springs inside, learn about springs, learn about wheels, and never mind "energy."
>
> Source: Richard P. Feynman. Surely You're Joking, Mr. Feynman! Adventures of a Curious Character. New York: W. W. Norton and Company, 1985. Print. 297–298.

What's the Big Idea?

Read this passage from Feynman's book carefully. What is its main idea? What evidence does he use to support his point? Come up with a few sentences showing how Feynman uses two or three pieces of evidence to support his main point.

CHAPTER TWO

How Do We Know about Energy?

Humans have known about energy for as long as they have existed. But people haven't always understood energy. The earliest people could feel the warm sunshine on their faces. They could see rivers flowing. They noticed plants growing. They watched animals running, swimming, and flying. They noticed the changes in nature and in themselves. They saw that things were always happening. And they

An ancient cave painting of a bison, which was found in Spain, shows ancient people's view of the natural world.

made things happen, too, by doing the work required to survive.

Over time, people have searched for new and better ways to do work. We have come up with many technologies to harness nature's power. This process has helped us understand energy better.

Energy Technologies through Time

Approximately 400,000 years ago, ancient people learned to control fire. This meant they figured out how to harness energy outside their bodies. Through burning plant and animal fuels, humans could release the chemical energy stored within fuels. People then used this energy to produce heat and light. Around 11,000 years ago, people began taming animals and using them to do work. They used the energy of animals to push, pull, carry, and more.

Later, humans realized they could harness other kinds of energy too. Wind pushed sailboats along Africa's Nile River as early as 5,000 BCE. By approximately 200 BCE, people across Asia were using windmills and waterwheels. Wind and waterpower, animal power, and fire were the key energy technologies through the 1600s CE.

In the late 1700s people began studying energy and developing new technologies. Benjamin Franklin proved that lightning was a form of electricity. Allesandro Volta invented the electric battery. James Watt built a coal-fired steam engine.

In the 1800s inventors in Europe and the United States perfected the gas-fired internal combustion engine, which is still used in cars. Engineers figured out how to create electricity using water, wind, and steam to power turbines. Engineers also created ways to send electricity over long distances.

What's a Watt?

People measure electricity in units called watts. Different machines need different amounts of watts to work. The term *watt* honors inventor James Watt. A laptop computer needs approximately 50 watts. A microwave oven needs approximately 750 to 1,100 watts. A hair dryer needs approximately 1,200 to 1,875 watts.

By 1900 humans were using energy at a rapid rate. In the mid-1900s, scientists came up with two new ways to produce power. One was nuclear power and the other was photovoltaics.

In the 1930s Italian physicist Enrico Fermi discovered that splitting a certain type of atom caused a chain reaction. The chain reaction released a huge amount of energy. Soon this technology was used in the world's first nuclear bomb in 1945 and nuclear power plant in 1951.

Scientists knew that sunlight shining on certain minerals could make electricity flow. In 1954 Bell Laboratories' researchers Daryl Chapin and Calvin Fuller created the first useful photovoltaic cell. This cell made enough electricity to run everyday electrical equipment.

Great Thinkers

Many great thinkers have helped us understand physics. Pythagoras, Leucippus, Democritus, and Epicurus were scholars in ancient Greece from the

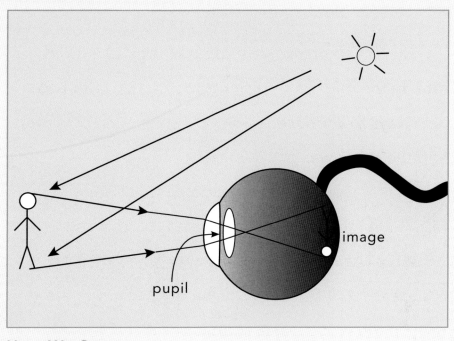

How We See

Compare how this diagram explains human sight with how the text does so. How are they similar? How are they different?

500s to the 200s BCE. They were the first to suggest that super-small atoms make up matter. They also said different combinations of atoms make up different materials.

Arab mathematician Hassan Ibn al-Haitham lived from 965 to 1040 CE and studied light. He said that we see because light enters our eyes. He said light travels in rays.

Albert Einstein's work changed the way we make and use energy.

English scholar Isaac Newton studied the laws of nature. He described the laws of motion very clearly in a book he published in 1687. He is especially famous for describing the law of gravity.

German-American physicist Albert Einstein developed several completely new ideas about matter and energy. Among other things, he proved that atoms exist. He showed that light acts like particles of matter in a paper he published in 1905. He proposed the idea of relativity. This idea says that the time you measure for any occurrence depends on your position and speed. Einstein's work led to many new technologies. These technologies include nuclear power, photovoltaics, television, lasers, and more.

Einstein on Relativity

Einstein knew relativity was confusing for ordinary people. To help them understand, he made a real-life comparison. He said that if you put your hand on a hot stove for a minute, it feels like an hour passes. But if you sit with a pretty girl for an hour, it seems like only a minute passes. That is what relativity is.

All kinds of people have developed new energy tools for human use. This quest continues today. Through it we've not only added to our options for energy use, but also learned a great deal about the nature of energy.

CHAPTER THREE

Kinetic Energy

Kinetic and potential are the two main forms of energy. Each form includes several different types. Kinetic energy includes the energy of objects, particles, and substances in motion.

Objects in Motion

Objects tend to do what they are doing, whether they are standing still or moving. If at rest, an object stays at rest. If in motion, an object stays in motion.

The energy from a racket moves to a tennis ball when it is hit.

Light from the sun travels in rays to reach the earth.

That changes when another force interacts with an object. A force can cause an object that is moving to stop. Or a force can cause an object that is still to start moving.

Particles in Motion

The motion of tiny particles is another type of kinetic energy. Electricity is one example of particles in motion.

All matter is made up of atoms. And atoms are made up of smaller particles such as protons,

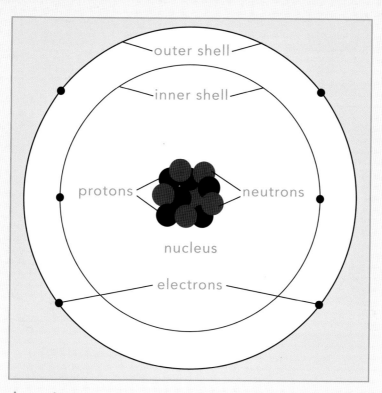

A Carbon Atom

This diagram shows the structure of a carbon atom. How is what is shown in the diagram different from how an atom is explained in the text? How is it similar?

neutrons, and electrons. Protons and neutrons cluster to form the nucleus of the atom. Electrons circle the nucleus in invisible shells. The shells are layered around the nucleus. Protons and electrons attract each other. This attraction holds the atom together. Electrons closest to the nucleus are strongly attracted to the protons. Electrons farther away may have a weaker attraction. Forces such as magnetism can move the outer electrons from one atom to another. When electrons move among atoms, they create a current of electricity.

Substances in Motion

The motion of substances is a third type of kinetic energy. Light, heat, and sound are all substances in motion.

Light is made of photons. Photons are bundles of energy. Photons travel in rays that move out in all directions. The photons travel along the rays in the form of a wave. We call it a wave because the energy alternates between high and low, like a water wave.

Devices at a Tokyo, Japan, railway station were tested in 2008 to produce electricity using the sound vibrations made as people walked through railway ticket gates.

Heat is the vibration of the atoms and molecules within a substance. The more the atoms vibrate, the hotter the substance gets. The motion of heat can do work and change matter.

Sound is a different kind of vibration. We sense that vibration with our ears. The motion of sound is a weak form of kinetic energy.

CHAPTER FOUR

Potential Energy

Several different types of potential energy exist too. Potential energy includes chemical, gravitational, elastic, and nuclear energy. All four types exist because of matter's position or how its parts are arranged.

Chemical Energy

Plants take in energy from sunlight, water, air, and soil. They store some of it as chemical energy. This energy

As plants grow, they store chemical energy from the sun's light.

exists in the bonds holding together the plants' atoms and molecules. Breaking those bonds releases the energy. The released energy can then do work. Eating is one way to break the bonds in food. Burning is another way to release chemical energy.

Gravitational Energy

Gravitational energy is another type of potential energy. It's energy an object has because Earth's gravity pulls it. Earth's gravity pulls everything on and near Earth.

When an object is lifted above Earth's surface, the lifting works against gravity. But gravity still pulls on the object. This gives the object gravitational energy. The higher and heavier the object, the more gravitational energy it has. If the lifter is removed, the object falls, slides, or rolls as low as it can go. Its gravitational energy is released.

Elastic Energy

Elastic energy is a third type of potential energy. When an object resists being stretched or squeezed out of shape, it has elastic energy. If you stretch a rubber band between your two hands, the rubber band resists. Stretching gives the rubber band elastic energy. If you let go with one hand, the rubber band goes flying. Letting go releases the elastic energy.

Nuclear Energy

Nuclear energy is yet another type of potential energy. It exists in the forces that hold an atom's nucleus together. Combining two or more atoms or splitting an atom's nucleus releases energy.

Superpower

Nuclear energy is very powerful. It's the richest source of energy in our universe, as far as we know. Just 1 pound (0.5 kg) of uranium can produce as much energy as 1 million gallons (3.8 million L) of gasoline. But, nuclear fission requires a rare fuel and creates waste that is hard to dispose. The waste must be contained and kept away from people.

Combining atoms is called fusion. Fusion happens inside the sun. The sun is a huge ball of gases, mostly hydrogen. Gravity holds the gases together, causing great pressure and heat. The hot atoms vibrate forcefully. They crash into one another at super-high speeds. This makes them gain and lose particles. The hydrogen atoms stick together. Their protons and electrons combine. This process changes hydrogen into helium. It also releases vast amounts of energy.

The process of splitting an atom is called fission. When humans engineer nuclear fission, they use the rare metals plutonium and uranium for fuel.

A plutonium nucleus is hit with a free neutron inside either a bomb or a nuclear reactor. The nucleus captures the neutron. The extra neutron makes the atom unstable. It splits into two smaller atoms. During this split, the atom throws off several neutrons. The thrown-off neutrons crash into other atoms. The other atoms split and release neutrons of their own. This creates a chain reaction. It also releases a lot of energy. Engineers can control the energy to create electricity.

EXPLORE ONLINE

The focus in Chapter Four was the different types of potential energy. It also touched upon nuclear energy. The Web site below focuses on nuclear energy. As you know, every source is different. How is the information given in the Web site different from the information in this chapter? What information is the same? How do the two sources present information differently? What can you learn from this Web site?

Energy Kids: Uranium (nuclear) Basics
www.eia.gov/kids/energy.cfm?page=nuclear_home

CHAPTER FIVE

Sunlight: Earth's Engine

Energy makes things happen in our universe. Every single event is the result of energy transfer. Through a constant series of energy transfers, the sun fuels nearly every process that happens on Earth. The energy from the sun radiates outward. Eventually that energy reaches the rest of the solar system, including Earth.

A mule deer gets energy from the plants it eats.

A Shrinking Baton

In a food chain, energy gets passed along like a baton. But the baton shrinks with each pass. A plant uses most of the solar energy it gets to live and grow. Only approximately 3 percent is stored as chemical energy in the plant. When an herbivore eats a plant, it doesn't get all that chemical energy. The herbivore may not eat the whole plant. It may not be able to digest some of what it eats. When a carnivore eats the herbivore, a similar energy shrinkage happens.

Sunlight into Food

Sunlight is the first link in every food chain on Earth. All plants get the energy they need through photosynthesis. Photosynthesis changes the kinetic energy of sunlight into the chemical energy of food.

The molecules of a plant contain chemical energy. Eventually another living thing uses that energy. An herbivore, such as a deer, might eat the plant. The deer digests the plant. This releases energy. The deer uses that energy to move and grow. A carnivore, such as a wolf, might then eat the deer.

Ethanol fuel can be used to power cars.

Or the deer might die naturally. The deer's body becomes food for bacteria.

Sunlight into Fuel

A plant can also become fuel. A person might burn wood for light and heat. Corn plants can be made into a fuel called ethanol. People can burn ethanol for light and heat or for powering machines. Fuel made from living plants is biofuel.

Coal, oil, and natural gas are fuels made by nature. They formed from ancient plants and animals buried underground. Over millions of years, heat and pressure changed the plants and animals into fuels packed with chemical energy. We call them fossil fuels

because they formed from fossils before the time of dinosaurs.

By burning a biofuel or fossil fuel, we change its chemical energy into kinetic energy. This energy can power a machine.

Sunlight into Weather

The sun also sets Earth's air and water in motion. The sun warms the land, oceans, and atmosphere to different temperatures. These temperature differences create ocean currents and weather. The word *weather* means conditions in Earth's atmosphere. These conditions include temperature, wind, and rainfall or snowfall.

Author and science professor Isaac Asimov wrote about the conservation of energy in his book *Isaac Asimov's Book of Science and Nature Quotations:*

> *The law of conservation of energy tells us we can't get something for nothing, but we refuse to believe it.*
>
> Source: Isaac Asimov and Jason Shulman. Isaac Asimov's Book of Science and Nature Quotations. *London, UK: Weidenfeld and Nicolson, 1988. Print. 75.*

Consider Your Audience

Read the passage above closely. How could you adapt Asimov's words for a different audience, such as your neighbors or your classmates? Write a blog post giving this same information to the new audience. What is the most effective way to get your point across to this audience? How is language you use for the new audience different from Asimov's original text? Why?

Motion into Megawatts

Earth is alive with kinetic energy. Nature produces many kinds of motion. Temperature differences cause winds to blow. Gravity helps rivers flow from high places to low places. People create many kinds of motion too. Our bodies are always on the go. And we've invented many machines that spin, swing, pump, and move in other ways.

Energy from the wind is turned into electricity through wind turbines.

Humans have also figured out how to harness motion—or transfer its energy—to get things done. We can move our muscles to do work. We can hitch horses to pull plows. We can use windmills to pump water. We can use waterwheels to run lumber sawmills. We can even turn motion into megawatts.

Turbines

A turbine is a tool often used to turn motion into electricity. An electrical turbine uses the motion of wind, water, or an engine to create an electrical current.

A wind turbine is one kind of electrical turbine. A wind turbine has three main parts: a rotor, a shaft, and a generator. The rotor looks like a fan or an eggbeater. It's a set of blades attached to a central piece called a hub. As wind pushes against the blades, they move. This movement makes the hub spin. The hub is attached to a rod called the shaft. As the hub spins, so does the shaft. The spinning shaft is attached to a generator that creates an electric current.

A water turbine creates electricity in a similar way. First, people build a dam on a river. The dam blocks the flow of water, making an artificial lake upstream. The lake is called a reservoir. People control the flow of water through openings in the dam. The openings contain turbines. The rotor of a water turbine may look like a propeller or a wheel. As the water flows over the turbines, they spin and create electricity.

People can also use the motion of a heat engine to make electricity. We can either boil water to make steam or heat a gas directly. As the steam or other

Geothermal Power Plants

Deep inside Earth, it's so hot that rocks melt. In places called hot spots, this heat escapes to the surface. Hot springs and geysers are places where water heated underground reaches the surface. Sometimes geothermal water reservoirs lie near Earth's surface. Geothermal power plants drill into the reservoirs and pump up hot water. Steam rising off that hot water turns turbines and creates electricity.

gas expands, it spins a turbine. The turbine then creates electricity.

As you can see, energy exists in many different forms. And as it changes from form to form and moves from place to place, it makes things happen. Energy is the engine that powers our whole universe.

FURTHER EVIDENCE

There is quite a bit of information about turbines in Chapter Six. It covered water and wind turbines. But if you could pick out the main point of the chapter, what would it be? What evidence was given to support that point? Visit the Web site below to learn more about turbines. Choose a quote from the Web site that relates to this chapter. Does this quote support the author's main point? Does it make a new point? Write a few sentences explaining how the quote you found relates to this chapter.

Energy Story: Chapter 6–Turbines, Generators, and Power Plants
www.energyquest.ca.gov/story/chapter06.html

Geothermal power plants use steam heated inside the earth to make power.

IMPORTANT DATES

400,000 years ago
Humans learn to control fire.

11,000 years ago
Humans begin taming animals.

5000 BCE
Earliest sailboats sail the Nile River.

500s–200s BCE
Ancient Greek scholars suggest that atoms make up matter and that different combinations of atoms make up different materials.

200 BCE
People across Asia use windmills and waterwheels.

965–1040 CE
Arab mathematician Hassan Ibn al-Haitham suggests that light travels in rays and that we see because light enters our eyes.

1687
Isaac Newton describes the laws of motion in his book.

1905
German-American physicist Albert Einstein publishes a paper that shows that light acts like particles of matter.

1930s
Italian physicist Enrico Fermi conducts the first successful experiment with splitting atoms.

1954
Scientists at Bell Laboratories create the first photovoltaic cell that makes enough electricity to run an ordinary electrical device.

OTHER WAYS YOU CAN FIND ENERGY IN THE REAL WORLD

Steam Engines

A steam engine is a kind of heat engine. It has six basic parts: a heat source, a boiler full of water, a valve, a cylinder, a piston, and a wheel. The heat source, such as a coal fire, heats the water to steam inside the boiler. As the steam escapes from the engine, a piston moves and powers a machine. You can see steam engines at the Steamtown National Historic Site in Scranton, Pennsylvania. Inside the museum, visitors can learn about the use of steam engines in trains.

Geothermal Hot Spots

Most of the world's geothermal hot spots lie in an area called the Ring of Fire. This area circles the Pacific Ocean. Most US geothermal power plants are in the western states and Hawaii. This is where geothermal groundwater is close to the surface. California generates the most electricity from geothermal energy. A geothermal power plant called the Geysers in California has been generating electricity since the 1960s.

Hybrid Cars

A hybrid vehicle such as the Toyota Prius runs on both an internal combustion engine and electricity. When the vehicle is traveling at low speeds, it uses its gas-burning engine. The engine's motion generates electricity. A battery stores this electricity. When the battery has been charged, the vehicle stops burning gas and runs on electricity instead. When battery power dips—or if the vehicle is traveling at a high speed and needs more energy than the battery can release—the internal combustion engine kicks in again.

Why Do I Care?

This book explains how different kinds of energy are used every day. List two or three ways that you use energy in your life. For example, what did you eat today? What machines did you use today?

Another View

Ask a librarian or another adult to help you find another source about energy. Write a short essay comparing and contrasting the new source's point of view with that of this book's author. Be sure to answer these questions: What is the point of view of each author? How are they similar and why? How are they different and why?

Surprise Me

Think about what you learned from this book. Can you name two or three facts about energy that you found most surprising? Write a short paragraph about each, describing what you found surprising and why.

Say What?

Studying about energy can mean learning a lot of new vocabulary. Find five words in this book you've never seen or heard before. Use a dictionary to find out what they mean. Then write the meaning in your own words, and use each word in a new sentence.

GLOSSARY

atmosphere
a mix of gases that surrounds
a planet

atom
the tiniest part of an
element that contains all the
properties of that element

carnivore
an animal that eats meat

herbivore
an animal that eats plants

kinetic
to do with motion or caused
by motion

megawatt
a unit of power equal to
1 million watts

molecule
a group of atoms in
a substance

nucleus
the central part of an atom

photosynthesis
a process that changes
sunlight into food

photovoltaics
the science of converting
sunlight directly
into electricity

potential
possible, but not yet actual

technology
the use of science to make
tools and do practical things

turbine
a device that harnesses
energy by spinning

LEARN MORE

Books

Boyle, Jordan. *Examining Wind Energy.*
　　Minneapolis, MN: Clara House Books, 2013.

Spilsbury, Richard and Louise. *Wind Power.*
　　New York: PowerKids Press, 2012.

Woodford, Chris. *Energy.* New York:
　　DK Publishing, 2007.

Web Links

To learn more about energy, visit ABDO Publishing
Company online at **www.abdopublishing.com**.
Web sites about energy are featured on our Book
Links page. These links are routinely monitored and
updated to provide the most current information
available.

Visit **www.mycorelibrary.com** for free additional tools
for teachers and students.

INDEX

ancient energy
   technologies, 12
Asimov, Isaac, 35
atoms, 14–17, 21, 23,
   25–29

Chapin, Daryl, 14
chemical energy, 7, 12,
   25–26, 32–33

Democritus, 15

Einstein, Albert, 16
elastic energy, 25, 27
electricity, 13–14, 20,
   22, 23, 29, 38–40
energy conservation, 6
engines, 13
Epicurus, 15

Fermi, Enrico, 14
Feynman, Richard, 9

fossil fuels, 33–34
Franklin, Benjamin, 13
Fuller, Calvin, 14

geothermal power
   plants, 39
gravity, 16, 25–26, 28,
   37

heat energy, 23, 33, 39

Ibn al-Haitham, Hassan,
   15

kinetic energy, 6–8,
   19–20, 22–23, 32, 34,
   37

Leucippus, 15
light energy, 6, 25, 31

Newton, Isaac, 16

nuclear energy, 14, 17,
   25, 26, 27–29

photons, 22
photosynthesis, 32
photovoltaics, 14, 17
potential energy, 6–8,
   19, 25
Pythagoras, 15

relativity, 17

turbines, 13, 38–40

Volt, Allesandro, 13

water energy, 13, 25,
   38–39
Watt, James, 13
watts, 13, 38
wind energy, 12–13, 38

ABOUT THE AUTHOR

Christine Zuchora-Walske has been writing and editing books and articles for children, parents, and teachers for more than 20 years. She has written books for children and young adults on science, history, and current events.